Drowned in a Silence of Ashes

Mahesh Kumar J

BlueRose ONE.com
Stories Matter
NewDelhi • London

BLUEROSE PUBLISHERS
India | U.K.

BlueRose ONE.com
Stories Matter
NewDelhi • London

For permissions requests or inquiries regarding this publication, please contact:

BLUEROSE PUBLISHERS
www.BlueRoseONE.com
info@bluerosepublishers.com
+91 8882 898 898
+4407342408967

ISBN: 978-93-7139-382-9

Cover design: Yash Singhal
Typesetting: Namrata Saini

First Edition: July 2025

Dedication

To the version of me that was broken,
shattered by betrayal,
burned by the hands I once held with love.

To the silence that screamed louder than pain,
and the ashes I rose from, piece by piece.

This is for the heart that kept beating
even when it had every reason to stop.

And to anyone who has ever been betrayed,
but chose to heal –
this book is your mirror,
your fire,
your quiet revolution.

– Mahesh Kumar J

Acknowledgements

To Amma and Acha, for loving me through every silence I couldn't explain.

To Chechi and my little nephew, for being light when I forgot how to carry my own.

To Maama, my silent supporter even from far away – your quiet presence meant more than words.

To all my Gurus and Maa for teaching me to turn pain into art and be stronger

To my late grandparents and Appachi, whose quiet blessings still follow me.

To my Sivakumar sir, Gabriel sir, Nimmy maam and Vijayakumar sir – for shaping the language I now bleed in.

To Uninked and Let's Write TVM, for being more than clubs – for being refuge.

To the quiet few I found later on, who became everything when I least expected – thank you for arriving, staying, and believing.

This book, Drowned in a Silence of Ashes, carries all of you in its bones.

With love,
Mahesh Kumar J

Preface

Before You Open These Pages

Some books are written with hope. This one was written with grief.

These words came from nights I didn't think I'd survive, from memories I couldn't bury, from love that left me both shattered and strangely whole.

This is not a story of a clean ending. It is a quiet scream, a soft prayer, a slow rebuilding.

If you've ever been left behind, loved too deeply, or stayed longer than you should have – this book might know you.

And if you're healing, even if you're still crawling then this is for you.

– Mahesh

Contents

Section 1

War and Wounds

1. Love in Times of War

No, we did not.
We did not grow apart.
But we did sharpen–
like swords turned into enemies.

No clean breaks,
only fractures beneath every word,
every apology, every sorry,
every crack in every quiet room we shared.

You were tired of holding me–
a hero without armor.
I forgot how to speak
without causing you pain.

We didn't argue–
we laid mines in each other's chests,
waiting for the wrong step.

I held you like a flag I swore to defend,
even as you burned it in front of me.
I healed every wound with trembling hands,
kissed the ash from your lips.
You spat it back in my mouth
and called it love.

Still, I stayed—
fighting ghosts of the girl you used to be,
begging shadows for answers.

You gave me silence,
then blamed me for not hearing you scream.
I called it war.
You called it over.

But you weren't done.
You summoned your reinforcements.
He arrived like a nation—
stronger, taller, broader,
his smile untouched by sorrow.

He didn't carry my guilt.
He hadn't slept on the floor
outside your locked door.
Hadn't seen the storm in your mind.

He touched you like a victory.
I touched you like a relic.
I was terrified to witness it—
and yet, I did.

You smiled finally.
Like peace had finally come.
He took your hand—
and with it, my war ended.

But peace never came for me.
I was captured.

Not by force,
but by your forgetfulness.

Your memory became my prison.
His shadow fell over me
like an execution order.

And they came for me—
your new world,
your better ending.
They dragged me through the wreckage
of all I built for you.

I begged with a voice you used to love.
You blinked.
That was all.

They hung me with a rope
spun from every apology
you never forgave.

He kicked me out.
You looked away—
in hatred,
in indifference.
As if I was already dead to you.

But as my breath left with the wind,
your tears finally broke—
a late rebellion.

You wept not for my death,
but for the love you never understood
until it could no longer answer.

And you realized–
he loves you like a soldier claims land.
I loved you like a refugee forgives home.

He will hold your victories.
I held your ruins.

2. *Snap of Fingers*

You moved on in the blink of an eye—
no goodbyes, no sorrow, no light.

Your voice cracked through the phone,
pouring poison like you owned my soul.

You hit me like a storm I couldn't weather,
shattered me piece by piece.

In your anger, I lost everything,
spiraled deep where demons were my only friends.

I drowned my pain in whiskey and smoke,
each puff a lie I told myself to cope.

Your laughter–
a cruel memory in my head,
while I bled inside, broken and betrayed.

You found happiness
in someone else's arms,
betrayed my trust
with your cold, cruel charms.

A knife in my back, with a smile.
You crossed miles now–
but not for me.

You shattered my world,
left me begging for answers,
on my knees.

And I, like a fool,
held you like a shrine.

Now I'm just ashes, fading in pain,
while you dance free in sunshine after rain.

You moved on
like it was nothing at all—
but I'm still here,
shattered, waiting to fall.

3. *Peace Was Signed in My Blood*

Here I am, standing tall–
Or standing lost?

Does being tall mean
you have nothing to weigh you down,
or simply that there's nothing left
to love you back?

You loved her.
You loved yourself.
But you believed loving yourself
meant loving her first.

If it was love,
why is the fort cracking?
Cracking, crumbling, left in ruins?

The walls echo arguments.
Windows shattered by misunderstandings.

Your betrayals.
Your coldest words–
"You lacked. So I chose what didn't."

Every morning, I woke up with hope.
Hope that the battle was over.
But battles with enemies
end in victory or defeat.

Battles with love
only end in heartbreak.

Because when you love someone,
you're willing to lose–
just to see them smile.

But them?
They wanted to win–
even if it meant watching me fall
so her new king could rise.

She was once my fellow soldier.
We fought side by side
against every enemy.

Now my allies watch in horror.
My enemies cheer.
And she–
she hangs me like a prisoner of war,
smiling as her new king slits my throat.

Little did I know–
she stopped showing up for battle.
Stopped wearing her armor.
Stopped answering our war cries.

And one day,
when an army stormed our fortress,
I saw her–
fighting against me.
Beside him.

Still, I fought.
Days. Weeks. Alone.
In denial.
In desperate hope
that the woman I fought every war for,
would remember why we built this fort.

But she wanted me dead.
My skull crushed.
Heart pierced.
My name erased
from every corner of the castle
we once danced in.

And the bullets?
They didn't come from strangers.
They came from you–
the hands that once held me,
the lips I once kissed.

You pulled the trigger from behind.
And somehow, that hurt worse
than any sword I'd ever known.

I wish it was him who killed me.
Then I could tell myself,
"I died because I wasn't enough."

But when you did it–
it wasn't rejection.
It was erasure.

And yet, in my final breath,
as my blood pooled at your feet,
I wished you peace—
with him. Or whoever comes next.

But not with me.
Not in this life.
Not in the next.
Not in any lifetime
where I might still ache for you.

I hope one day you cry with him too—
not from pain,
but from overwhelming gratitude,
the way you did
when the world was against you
and I whispered:
"It's okay. These shoulders will protect you
until blood stops running in me."

4. Silent Minefields

Yes, the battle ended–
She chose to leave.
Leave with grace,
as she calls it.

But here I am,
looking down from the sky
at my lifeless body–
slit open, fed to the dogs,
bleeding, yet skin and bone,
flesh even vultures won't taste.

I look again and see no body–
only the fights,
the betrayals,
the heartbreak.

How you left
when my demons took me over–
the same ones I exorcised from inside you
when they ate you alive.

But when they came for me–
you chose to be yourself.
You chose to leave.

And I was left,
demons exacting final revenge,
dragging me under one last time.

I am alone in a battlefield
that looks quiet after war,
yet deadly beneath the surface.

My life has left my body—
but not my soul.
It still searches for you,
the mate it longs for.

Here I am, trying to move on
into a new realm,
while my soul lingers,
each step taken with caution,
like a warlord.

Each step risks opening wounds
that never healed—
explosions of pain,
memories, regrets,
unsaid words,
silences louder than any scream.

The wounds are no longer visible—
only invisible scars,
detonating slowly, painfully.

A constant minefield of betrayal.

Each shadow in this field
haunted by men lost in wars
holds a memory,
frozen like photos in a gallery.

I wish silence was peace.
But it isn't.
It's a minefield.

One wrong move,
one thought,
one memory,
one feeling of missing you–
can shatter me again.

And yet I wonder–
Is there still a heart at all?
Or has it been blown apart
too many times to count?

Does it beat for me–
or for the world?

And there I see you–
in your favorite lehenga,
with your jhumkas and bangles,
celebrating victory with your new warrior.

While I am torn between my grave,
where my soul is buried,
and the sky,
where my life longs to ascend.

And yet, like a fool,
I dance in this battlefield,
hoping to hear your war cry again—
for you, for me,
to come and save you.

5. *Chaos After the War*

She said it like a joke–
how he held her throat like a wine glass,
how the headboard knocked like a war drum,
while I lay awake at 2 a.m.,
smoking, crying,
trying to banish the image–

Her limbs folded into someone else's shadow,
the choreography we once made
now danced by him and her.

She sips chai with him now
at the same shop
where we once held love in our hands.

Calls it her "little ritual."
And I wonder if he knows
she called me her morning prayer once.

When our knees touched under café tables
and I told her
the world could end right then
and I'd be okay with her by my side.

They went on my old route–
that highway, those beaches,
those late-night drives
where she once cried in my arms,

after telling me
no one loved her like I did.

Now she rides pillion, laughing,
head tilted back,
hair kissing wind–
as if none of that ever happened.

Her eyes sparkled when she whispered,
"He made me feel so good I saw God,"
and I died for the third time that week.

She said he made her feel
like lightning–
not like the quiet rain I was,
always waiting,
apologizing,
afraid to do too much.

She said I was soft–
like a poem with no teeth.
Too slow. Too safe.

That I felt like dead air.
That my belly was "warm but sad,"
like an old man's lullaby.

I looked in the mirror after that–
motionless strands twisting out of place,
belly a map of every failure I fed,
eyes red from wars
I never even got to fight.

She watches sunrises now
from the same cliff
we carved our names into.

I sit on the bathroom floor,
fingers clutched around my phone
like a grenade I can't throw,
scrolling through all the new pictures—
like a soldier rewatching war footage.

But it's not me.
And I tell myself that over and over,
hoping this time,
I'll survive it.

Section 2

Grief and Hollow Spaces

1. When Death Becomes Tender

I wish that one day,
someone will see this–
maybe a human,
maybe an animal,
maybe that power above.
But if they all refuse to,
if they choose to watch me suffer,
cry and crawl like a man–
a man who lost his ability to walk–
then let it be.

Because my will to live doesn't even live anymore.
So at least then,
when Death comes to me,
she will say the things
I yearned to hear in life–

"Sorry for not being the shoulder to put my head on."
"Sorry for leaving you alone."
"Sorry for always victimizing you."
"Sorry for telling you your truth never mattered."
"Sorry for disregarding your emotions."

And finally, she hugs me and whispers,
"I wish we met earlier,
so we could create more memories before we part."

But I look at her and ask,
“My beloved–
take me forever to the eternity you promised.
For I will be your companion.”

And Death smiles,
“Yes, come to me. I am always here for you.”

I look back–
at my lifeless body,
with monitors beeping all around.
And I smile and think to myself,
"Aren’t these the exact words
I yearned to hear all my life?"

2. The Villain They Needed

They all watched me bleed–
quietly,
some with popcorn,
others with pity
they wore like perfume.

She told the story first,
and louder.
Painted herself in soft pastels–
the broken girl
who tried her best.
And me?
I was the monster
who made her cry.

Never mind the nights
I held her shaking body
like it was sacred.
Never mind the way
I stitched her soul
while mine was unraveling.

No one asked for my version.
No one wanted
the truth if it meant
loving me too.

They needed me to be
the villain—
it made their dinner conversations easier.

"She's healing," they said.
"She deserves love."
As if I didn't.
As if what I felt
was disposable rage,
not grief burning at the seams.

They whispered about my anger,
never the years I bit my tongue.
They called me bitter,
not broken.

And gods—
how they loved her.
Still do.
Still post her selfies.
Still invite her in.
Still say,
"She's important.
She's changed."

And me?
I'm just the cautionary tale
they never quote fully.
The one who loved too much,
lost too much,
and screamed too late.

But if I'm a monster–
it's only because
they built me one
brick by brick,
lie by lie,
until even I
couldn't find the boy
beneath the fury.

3. *The Sun That Never Returns*

It feels heavy yet light at this hour–
I stand alone, stripped of all power.
The sun bleeds red, a fading sight,
in the silence, only my beliefs lie.

What I once believed could lift me to the top
is now a cruel joke of truth
a mockery in its purest form.

The sea listens to my woes.
I have myself but none to share.
Each one a silent call for help
as I come closer to the doom I always felt.

Hands that once held me–
now just footprints in the sand.
No one to trust.
No one to understand.

They come when it's pretty,
but they leave
when I'm at my lowest.
They say,
"You're not who I thought you were,"
when I get vulnerable–when I disappoint.

For love's a transaction
with a mask on its face–

a fleeting connection.
What a disgrace.

When the sun sets, I sigh–
another day passed
without me
saying goodbye to myself.

And so I stand at the cliff–
a lone silhouette.
But even that fades
once the sun sets.

With every dream shattered,
and only regrets embraced,
I hope that one day, just one day,
I will be the sun that sets–
and never returns.

So they'll know
how much light
I truly was.

4. The Room That Forgot My Name

This room once knew me
like a favorite sweater–
worn, soft, stretched at the edges,
smelling of rain and masala chai.

Now it coughs me out
like a foreign object stuck in the throat.

The couch remembers
how we curled–
knees tangled, your breath on my collar.
Now another body sighs into that space,
and the cushions don't call me back.

The mirror above the sink–
it used to watch you brush my hair.
Now it reflects a new outline,
your laughter tilting toward someone else.

Your mug still lives on the shelf,
cracked at the lip–
where I once kissed it like a substitute.

You brew coffee for someone else now.
The silence doesn't echo the same.

The playlist we built–
I know it still exists,
but I don't know what's on it anymore.

It plays,
but the lyrics mean nothing.
No one sings the chorus like I did.

There's a dent in the wall
where your words hit–
from the times you said
I never spoke with certainty.

You probably painted over it.
But I still see it.
And only I see it.

Your room forgot my name.
The sheets don't know my scent.
The desk drawer doesn't creak
in my frequency anymore.

But the walls–
they haven't moved.
They still lean in,
listening for my footsteps.

And at night,
when everything else sleeps,
they release my shadow
onto the floor.

The rooms may forget,
but the walls
still carry my voice.

5. The Saviour in Disguise

People leave quietly–
no slammed doors,
no final texts.

Just silence thickening
like fog on a windshield
as I drive home from work –
down the lonely road,
crying so hard the streetlights flicker.

Still–
not one call.
Not one voice asking,
"Are you okay?"

They say I'm the problem.
They always do.
Maybe I am.

Because I stopped pretending.
Because I needed more than fake care.
Because I cracked open
and no one stayed
to hold the pieces.

So I found a friend
in a little roll of fire–

a cigarette clutched
between my shaking fingers.

My first taste of stillness.
The first time I could breathe
without needing to earn it.

People prayed for my disappearance.
They threw blame like stones:
"You're too much."
"You're too weak."
"You're always playing victim."

And they walked away–
as if I wasn't worth saving.

I didn't scream.
I didn't beg.

But I did climb
the cracked stairs to my terrace,
stood at the edge,
as the wind whispered
like an old friend.

One more step.
One last leap.
One less burden in this world.

But the cigarette lit itself in my hand,
and I sat down instead.

I smoked like it was a prayer–
an offering to a world

that gave me nothing
except the curl of this smoke.

No gods came.
No warmth returned.
But the smoke stayed.

It stayed
when even memory tried to leave.

Call it weakness.
Call it poison.
But for me,
it was the only thing that listened.

My saviour,
in disguise.

Section 3

The Want to be Wanted

1. My Life is a Museum

My life is a museum–
of people letting me go that easily,
as if I were a postcard they picked up
and forgot to mail.

I wish, in another life,
someone fights for me.
Valiantly.
Burns bridges.
Kills men.
With swords, arrows,
and the fire of love and passion–
not just convenience.
Not lust wearing the mask of love.

For once,
I want to know someone would
raise armies and fight for me–
not just walk with me when the road is easy,
but stand guard at the gates
when my mind becomes a battlefield.

Fight against my abductors,
my countless inner demons
who come wearing old faces
and whispering old shames.

I want someone
who sees the war behind my smile,
who doesn't flinch at the ruins I carry,
but says:
"I see it. I'll stay."

Someone who doesn't run
the first time I fall apart,
but gathers the broken bits
and builds me shelter.

Is it too much
to want to be someone's reason
to stay,
to try,
to fight?

Because I've been the sanctuary
for too many wanderers–
the safe place they leave
once they're whole.

But gods–just once,
I want to be
the home that's never abandoned.
The museum someone chooses
to live inside.

2. The Guest Room in Their Heart

I was never a home–
just a guest room
in the grand hotel of their loneliness.

Neatly kept.
Convenient.
Forgettable.

They came in with tired hands,
turned lies into lullabies,
left their sorrows like used towels
on the soft chest of my silence.

I served without asking.
Folded my pain like linen,
hid my hopes
under bedsheets they never touched.

They used my kindness
like warm water–
to rinse off someone else's scent.

Told me I was safe,
but never stayed
when the night stretched to 3 a.m.
and my heart cracked open.

I kept their secrets like spare keys,
waited for the day
they might call me home.

But they left–
quietly,
leaving only
the echo in the hallway
and my scent in their collar.

And now the door stays open–
just in case.

Even if I know
I was never the destination.
Only the pit stop.

I am not
anyone's emergency contact.
Not someone
they fear losing.

But gods,
how I ache
to be someone's forever address–
someone's map-marked "stay"

3. *Would You Still Love Me on the Bathroom Floor?*

Would you still love me
if you saw the version of me
the world was too proud to see?

Not the one who smiles for photos,
makes playlists, buys coffee,
takes you to hilltops and talks about stars–
but the one collapsed on cold bathroom tiles,
blood running down like confessions
no god ever heard.

Would you still choose me
when I shake like a child
who was never held right,
crying so hard
my lungs turn inside out,
and I whisper to no one,
"I don't want to die,
but I can't live like this either."

Would you touch me
when my skin smells of metal and salt,
when my eyes have no light left,
and the only thing that's soft
is the sound of me breaking again?

Would you still want me
when I'm not strong,
not composed,
not a poem—
just a human mess
with a knife on the floor
and a scream in my throat?

Because I don't need
a saviour.

I need someone
who sees me drowning
and doesn't walk away
because the water is ugly.

I want a love
that kneels beside the blood,
presses their forehead to mine
while my chest heaves in silence,
and says—
"Even here, even now, you are mine."

4. What Wasn't Enough

I was the quiet architect
of her healing–
built her a home from my wounds,
stitched her childhood fears
into lullabies.

I showed her how to feel again.
Taught her to breathe without shaking.
Took her to the ocean
and said:
"See? The tide returns. So can you."

I kissed her forehead,
never raised my voice.
Taught her poems
from the tip of my tongue
until she wrote again.

She said she'd forgotten
how to smile before me.
I taught her that too.

Introduced her to every friend I had–
told them,
"This is the one."
Held her in moonlight,
never asked for thanks.

Never let her cry alone.
Made her body sing,
even when mine was tired.

And still–
the final word
wasn't love,
but the sound of her voice
describing his body
inside hers.

How he filled her
like thunder.

And I?
I was a drizzle
she didn't feel anymore.

No one asked what I did.
Only believed what she said.
And when they left,
they took her side–
and every piece of me I gave her.

Now she thrives.
And I?
Am just the man
who healed her
for someone else.

5. *Disposable*

I used to beg
to be heard–
voice skipping like a heartbeat
in a dying radio,
while they danced
to her version of the story.

No one asked for my truth.
No one noticed the blood
I wiped from my own mouth–
biting it shut
to keep her name clean.

They said,
"Get over it."

As if healing
were an app you update.
As if rage and grief
were software glitches
in an otherwise functioning man.

And when I tried to scream,
they shut the door and said–
"You're just like the rest of men."

But I'm not.
I wasn't.

I gave until my own reflection
started looking unfamiliar.

I want to be wanted–
not because I'm convenient,
not because I'm easy to silence
or good at being "low maintenance,"
but because someone looks at me
and thinks:
"Even his broken pieces are beautiful."

Not as a temporary fix
till someone shinier appears.
Not the screen protector
peeled off
once the new model arrives.

I want to be felt
in the silence after laughter.
I want my absence to ache
in the air like unfinished music.

I want someone to say–
"He was here, and it meant something."

And maybe now,
in quiet corners
where two kind strangers speak gently,
or a girl lights a cigarette
and doesn't ask me to shrink–
I feel it.

The faintest flicker.
A maybe.
A whisper.
Not of love,
but of being seen.

And gods,
that is enough for now.

Section 4

Moving on Quietly

1. You should wish yourself

At 11 pm, I cracked the silence–
a fragile thread I dared to pull.
"Happy birthday," I whispered,
like a ghost lost in the dark.

You asked me how I am–
I hid the bruises beneath my words.
The intense spirals, the lies–
but it was my heart breaking again.

You sighed relief,
and told me
"Hey, you should wish,
happy birthdays to yourself,
A new you is born"
I asked how you were–
"Not bad, not good. Great"
your voice crackled,
But I prayed to all gods,
that you be alright.

"I will care for myself,
Just like you taught me how I can be loved, beloved"

We ended the call–
words sinking like dead weight,
and I stood in the echo,
alone with the quiet,
watching the distance stretch
between what was
and what never will be.

But that's okay,
You tried, they tried too.
Somethings are beautiful,
Just the way they are.

2. *Some Loves Teach You to Let Go*

I'm caught between
becoming someone new
and staying broken
just to remember you better.

Every time I try to heal,
my mind runs barefoot
back to you–
bruised, bleeding,
yet smiling,
like a dog returning
to the hand that hurt it,
because once,
it was also the hand that fed.

You might have stabbed me
in the ways only soulmates know–
precise. Poetic.
And that's okay.

Because some part of me believed
if I bled enough,
you'd call it devotion
but it was my delusion.

I thought real love
meant enduring the storm.

But with you,
I was the storm.
And for that, I am deeply sorry,

Truly, madly, deeply,

Just like the song from Savage Garden.

Even now,
when I lie awake at 3:16 a.m.,
listening to my own heartache
echo through hollow ribs—
I wish you find happiness.

Real, raw ones.

And I?

I want to move on.
I do.
But my soul still makes space
for the idea of you—
still lights a candle
in the temple
of a love that never prayed back.

But, I have to.

Love doesn't mean,
holding on to someone,
Even if it bleeds them.
Sometimes loves is the strength
Strength to let go,

And be content with it,
Happy knowing,
That you still are the reason,
They are happy,
Because you chose to let it go,
And see them smile,
Just like you always wanted,
To see them smile wide open.

3. Outgrowing the Word 'Friend"

We said goodbye like grown-ups–
calm words,
clean break–
the kind you write about
in movies.

You said,
"best friends"
I said "best past"
Because I am honoring what it was,

Without staying behind its mask.

But that night, when I sang
for you, when you cried,

you hung up
the second someone else called.

I waited–
watched the clock
until it struck 3:30 a.m.
and struck me harder:

Its hard, to be friends with someone,

With whom you shared,

What no lovers did.

And maybe that's okay too,
Its going to hurt,
But it will be the norm.
And it must be.

How else would you honour that beautiful past?
Without having some walls up.
I am not lying, it hurts.
But I have to swallow the hurt one day.
And get myself better too.

You were a page, in my life.
A strong but beautiful page.
And I will now turn it, without bitterness,
But gratitude
And tonight, I will sleep,
Not to escape,
But to rest.
In the quiet corner of my room,

The same place I used to cry.

4. Watchpoint

I'm waking up
before the sun does now.
Lacing my shoes
instead of breaking again.

My body moves–
sore and slow–
but it moves.

Pickleball.
Badminton.
Sweat instead of sobbing.
Gym mirrors reflect
something almost strong–
almost me.

New people.
New laughs.
Friends who smoke with me
without asking if I'm okay,
because somehow,
they already know.

And my buddies who,
still play badminton with me,
With more happiness,
as I don't cry anymore.

The people who listened to my stories,
Watching me get better,
as in the movies.

I even sing now.
Alone.
In cafes and beaches,
where once
my voice was only a cry.
But somethings remain,
And its best left unsaid.
Because not everything,
will have a closure.
And that's okay too.

This world doesn't offer,
soft landings for men like me.
Just hard ground
and the guilt
for feeling anything at all.

Still–
my worst days are over.
I didn't jump.
Didn't vanish.
Didn't let the goodbye
write my ending.

This is my watchpoint–
where I look back
only to remember

I made it through the fire
without burning out.

And maybe–just maybe–
someday soon,
I'll forget how your name
tastes in my mouth.

Maybe not today.
But soon.

And when I do,
I will thank you,

For without you, I would not have grown.
You are the stepping stone.

5. The Last Thing I'll Ever Write About You

There were nights
I clawed my chest open
just to feel something real–
because your love
was a ghost that slept beside me
but never stayed till morning.

You wrecked me
like a storm that called itself mercy.
Smiled while I drowned.
Held my face like a blessing,
then kissed me like a curse.

You stitched your grief
into my skin,
told me to wear it
like it was ours,
then walked away
as if it never belonged to you.

And I let you.
Again.
And again.
And now, I write letters,
Not to what broke me,

But to whats coming.
You were a storm,
But I?
I am the sky that cleared itself.
And embraced the storm with grace.

One day,
I will meet someone who chooses me,
And no, its not your fault
That you didn't.
We are a different mess,
And we deserve ,
Different messes too.
Haha ! That's the first time,
My poem makes me laugh.
And not cry.
And I will meet a love, that stays
That listens when I whisper
And laughs when I do.
Not perfect, but present
Not loud, but in the moment.

This poem isnt about you,
Its about me,
How I faced the storm and still survived it.
That version is finally free.

And I finally hope, I can fix myself.
So this is it—
the last thing
I'll ever write
about you.

I wish you all success.
Happiness.
Kids who love you.
May you get your dream job,
And everything you desire.
And please fix yourself,
not for me,
but for the world,
to see how beautiful you are,
When you are completely healed
Goodbye.

Thank you,
For being my best memory,
and My best lesson.